Contents

Careers in Languages

your questions and answers

edited by

Nick Higgins

TROTMAN

This second edition published in 2002 in Great Britain by Trotman and Company Limited, 2 The Green, Richmond, Surrey TW9 1PL

© Trotman and Company Limited 2002

British Library Cataloguing in Publication Data

A catalogue record for this book is available from the British Library

ISBN 0 85660 773 8

Typeset by Palimpsest Book Production Limited, Polmont, Stirlingshire

Printed and bound in Great Britain by Bell & Bain (Scotland) Ltd

What about working in languages?

Wanting to work with languages is a very popular ambition. It sounds glamorous and exciting – as though there is lots of foreign travel involved. It also sounds as though there are plenty of jobs for linguists, given that we regularly read about the fact that the British are still behind other nationalities when it comes to learning foreign languages – and after all we are now part of a single European market which includes over 320 million inhabitants who do not speak English as their first language. You could be tempted to think that if you are one of the minority who *do* have a flair for languages and are willing to learn one or two, then the world should be your oyster.

However, the fact is that there are very few jobs for people who are good at languages *alone*. Languages must, in most cases, be seen as a secondary skill. This means that allied to other skills, they are very useful indeed and can enhance your job prospects in almost every area. If you think about it, language is a means of communication – but is not an end in itself. You would not get a job based solely on your ability to speak English. You would need other skills and aptitudes too.

Languages as a primary skill come into their own in three major career areas: teaching, interpreting and translating. We will look at these – and at other careers using languages – in this book.

What sorts of jobs are there?

First of all, the obvious ones. Those which use languages as a main skill are interpreting or translating on behalf of other people or teaching other people to communicate in a language. Even they, however, demand other qualities, as we shall see.

Interpreting

Interpreters' use of language is verbal. They translate orally, at a very high level and often at great speed, for individuals who cannot speak each others' language well enough to conduct the business in hand. They may translate into and from several languages.

There are three main styles of interpreting. Some interpreters prefer to offer one kind of service. Others enjoy and are competent in more than one.

Simultaneous interpreting involves translating speech almost as soon as it is uttered. Interpreters often sit in booths at international conferences, wearing headphones, and translate a speech as it is being made by one delegate. Other delegates, also wearing headphones, therefore hear the speech in their own language.

Consecutive interpreting is another technique. The interpreter makes notes of what is being said, often for several minutes, judges a suitable time to speak and then translates what has just been said. This technique is often used in smaller meetings.

Liaison interpreting is a combination of both methods. It is usually 'live' with the interpreter sitting or standing with a very small group of people or between just two. The interpreter waits until a few sentences have been spoken, then translates. This is the kind of interpreting that goes on when presidents, royalty and important people meet together or are seated next to one another for a meal and need to be able to converse. It is also used when visitors are being shown premises or when two or more people are holding a meeting.

Community interpreting is a new but expanding field. Interpreters are employed by courts, police services and government agencies to translate in case of difficulty. Often, this involves use of ethnic minority languages.

Some interpreters also translate – although this is quite a different skill – or teach part-time.

Translating

Translators *write* – they do not get much opportunity to *speak* other languages. They may of course, speak to clients in their own languages and may make phone calls or consult other linguists over the wording of a piece of text, but normally they use the written word.

It is normal practice, unless they are very, very fluent, for translators to translate from foreign languages into their own – known as their mother tongue. Most clients would not employ anyone offering to work the other way round – if you have ever grappled with instructions on how to use a product written in less than clear English, this is probably because the product comes from another country and the words have been translated by someone who is not thoroughly at home in the language. A good knowledge of their own language, of its grammar and nuances, is almost as important for a translator as knowledge of foreign languages.

Literary translation is a very small and specialised field, nearly always done by freelance (self-employed) translators.

Teaching

We all know what language teachers do – at school level that is. They help students to acquire the four skills of language: listening, speaking, writing and reading. In schools they teach all four. They may or may not, depending on the level they are working at and the demands of the syllabus, also teach current affairs, European studies or literature, rather like an English teacher does.

Other teachers, however, may concentrate on one particular skill. If they are employed in a language school which teaches adults they may have pupils who want to develop their speaking skills and perhaps improve their ability to use the telephone. Or they may have pupils who want to improve their written skills. Usually, they ask the pupils exactly what their needs are, then conduct an audit or test the level of skill they have already before devising a programme. Often they are required to teach specialised vocabulary or perhaps to help clients learn how to give a sales presentation in their chosen language. If they are preparing clients to go and live and work abroad they will also teach them about the culture and customs to expect.

One form of teaching which often interests people who are good at languages, but which does not strictly demand any knowledge of foreign languages, is that of teaching English to speakers of other languages – known as TEFL or Teaching English as a Foreign Language. Although the main skill required is that of teaching English well, people who have studied other languages (not necessarily the ones of their students) are usually good at doing this. They know the problems of learning other languages and the traps and pitfalls, through having gone through a similar process themselves.

Languages as a secondary skill

Secretarial work

Languages are of prime importance to some secretaries and personal assistants.

Secretaries who can use other languages do as much language work as their job requires. They may simply type the occasional letter, or may be the only person in the office who speaks any languages. A truly bilingual or trilingual secretary may be responsible for much of the correspondence, translate documents and letters, make all the phone calls requiring languages, meet, greet and entertain visitors – act as a combination of secretary and interpreter/translator in fact. They may also take dictation in a foreign language, using foreign shorthand, and may work for a manager whose first language is not English, 'tidying up' and polishing his or her English in any correspondence.

Government service

The British civil service has some departments where knowledge of languages is particularly useful. These include the Diplomatic Service (Foreign and Commonwealth Office), whose staff are posted to work in embassies and consulates in different countries, the Government Communication Headquarters and Joint Technical Language Service, where translators translate and analyse specialist (and sometimes secret) material, the Department of Trade and Industry, and the Customs and Immigration Services. The European civil service employs British nationals in Brussels, Luxembourg and Strasbourg.

Civil servants are first and foremost administrators (and in the case of diplomatic staff, representatives, presenting a favourable image of Britain abroad and promoting/explaining government policy). The European institutions also employ a separate class of specialists who work as translators and interpreters.

Travel and tourism

Many jobs in this field require knowledge of other languages, whether used to help British holidaymakers overseas or visitors to Britain from other countries.

Examples of jobs include:

- Steward/Stewardess – on an aircraft, ship or the international trains travelling through the Channel Tunnel
- Travel agency assistant
- Tourist Information Centre assistant

- Travel guide
- Representative or courier for a tour operator.

Sales and marketing

It is very important to be able to speak to customers in their own language. A customer is in charge and has the upper hand. He or she has an added advantage if negotiating in his or her own language. Psychology (and politeness) dictate that the marketing manager who is fluent in the customer's language gains some of the bargaining power.

Commerce, finance and industry

Many firms are now international or multi-national in outlook and operation. Many act for clients in other countries and have branch offices in many cities. It is not unusual now for major firms of accountants and lawyers to ask job applicants which languages they speak.

Other areas

Other jobs in which languages can be a valuable extra skill include:

- Journalism
- Information science and librarianship
- Hotel, catering and leisure management
- The media.

There are very few jobs in which languages are not an asset and many professions can be carried out abroad, giving people who speak languages the chance to travel and work in other countries. The range is enormous – from engineering to nursing; banking to environmental work; pharmacy to computing.

What qualifications will I need?

In the case of jobs for which languages are a secondary skill, you will, of course, have to first qualify professionally for your main work. The level of language required will then determine the type of qualification you will need, or if indeed you need any at all. Many travel reps and couriers for example have no formal qualifications in languages. They may have worked abroad, perhaps as an au pair, and picked up a sufficient knowledge for their work.

For the main linguistic jobs, however, you will almost certainly have to take a course of some kind.

Why *almost* certainly? Because a career using languages does not, strictly speaking, require any formal qualifications. It is not a profession like nursing or accountancy where you are required by law to have specific qualifications in order to practise. There are some very able linguists who earn a living without having done any kind of training. BUT they are usually either truly bilingual, having spoken two languages from birth, or have spent many years living in a different country and have acquired excellent language skills that way.

Most people need to study languages first to a high level of competence, such as a degree, and then they take a further course of training to learn how to apply them in a job. There are, however, exceptions again. While many people, for example, take a languages degree course then follow this with a course specially geared for translators or interpreters, there are other people who manage to establish themselves without doing the second course.

TEFL work normally demands a course of some kind but the only career for which you *must* have done a particular kind of training is that of a teacher in a state school. All such teachers must have taken a course at degree level which gives them qualified teacher status – either a BEd or one-year PGCE.

However good your knowledge of languages you may find that in order to give yourself credibility in the eyes of employers and/or clients it helps to become a member of a recognised professional language association such as the Institute of Linguists or the Institute of Translation and Interpreting. This usually requires you to pass their own examinations or to be able to demonstrate an equivalent level of competence. (Full details may be obtained direct from them – see address at the back of this guide.) Membership can help to put your name before prospective employers. Members of the Institute of Translation and Interpreting, for instance, have their names and addresses listed in a directory which is made available to people requiring translation and interpreting services.

What personal skills and attitudes are needed?

You would need to be accurate and able to pay attention to detail. Reliability is important. No-one wants to employ anyone who cannot produce work on time. Many jobs would bring you into contact with confidential information – especially if you were working in government offices or were handling sensitive translation work, so discretion is important.

You may need to be flexible and ready to work long or irregular hours. For instance, in the travel and tourism industry guests do not require your services between the hours of nine and five only. Reps have to escort holidaymakers to airports at all hours. Tour guides are often busiest at weekends. Teachers have lessons to prepare and mark. Translations are often required at very short notice.

In most jobs connected with languages you are going to be in constant contact with other people – colleagues, clients or pupils. You need to be a good communicator and able to relate well to all kinds of people.

Teachers must genuinely enjoy teaching and passing on their skills to others. It may sound obvious, but there are people who have trained to teach as a means of staying in a language-oriented environment, only to find on entering a classroom that they are not really cut out for it after all.

Stamina is a vital requirement for interpreters. Sitting in a conference booth concentrating totally can be very draining. And no interpreter can afford lapses in concentration.

If you were going to become a self-employed translator, then you would need to be good at managing your time and to be self-disciplined. You would also need to be able to market yourself effectively and set a rate for your services that fairly reflects the amount of work and time involved.

How competitive
an area is it?

There are very few opportunities to become a translator or interpreter available, and those that do exist require extremely high levels of linguistic ability, as well as written and oral skills. You will find that if this is where your ambitions lie, you will have to work extremely hard and rely heavily on perseverance – and no small amount of luck – to succeed. It is possible, but it may take significant time and effort.

Having said this, if you would prefer to use your aptitude for languages in a more general sense, then the competition is nowhere near as intense. The large number of languages degree courses available, for example, makes it relatively easy for you to find your way on to one. And a comparative shortage of language teachers means that it is currently a good area for budding linguists and/or teachers to get into.

In fact, if you consider using languages as a secondary skill then you actually gain a competitive edge over your rivals. Firstly, more jobs become physically available to you in the country whose language you can speak. And, secondly, an additional – very well respected – skill will always stand you in good stead when applying for positions in any career area.

What are the good and bad aspects of the work?

One bonus is that you will probably meet a lot of different people. Another is that you may get the chance to travel or to live in another country for a period.

There are downsides too. Working with a variety of people inevitably means that you will not get on with them all. You can't always change jobs or find new clients if the first ones are not compatible.

Another possible drawback is that in industry and commerce promotion prospects are limited for linguists. They are usually part of a small translation unit and the number of senior positions is not great.

Where will I work?

Your choice of place of work is as broad as the number of different jobs available. Linguists work for organisations of all shapes and sizes and you could find yourself in any number of environments, from the corridors of power of government, to the offices of huge multinational companies, to a noisy classroom, to your own home. And, of course, you needn't limit yourself to working in the UK.

Your options increase further still when you consider the number of places you could work using languages as a secondary skill. This incorporates virtually every working environment imaginable – there are very few jobs for which language skills are not a bonus.

Who will I work with?

Almost anyone. It depends entirely on the kind of work you choose and the kind of employer you work for. In industry and commerce you could work with directors, sales managers, marketing managers, bankers, lawyers, production managers, advertisers, clients, as well as other linguists.

In government work, you would spend your time among civil servants, politicians, high level diplomats, VIPs, translators and interpreters – of all nationalities.

In teaching you would spend most of your time with your pupils. For a secondary school teacher this means mainly teenagers – although they also work with colleagues and have contact with their pupils' parents. Other teachers specialise in teaching adults and work with students from all walks of life who want to learn languages for pleasure or for use with business clients. If you work for private language organisations you may spend part of your time visiting managers to establish what a company's requirements are before beginning classes for staff.

Some translators work mainly alone or with a small group of other linguists in a translation bureau.

Wherever you work, however, your immediate colleagues will be people who share your interest in languages.

What will I
earn?

There is no simple answer, as 'language work' describes more than one job. With one or two exceptions, linguists are not like, for example, medical professionals or civil servants who are paid on set salary scales and move to higher ones as they are promoted.

Having said that, career linguists in government service are paid on set scales, as are teachers in state schools. Teachers' salaries vary according to how long they have been working and whether they hold positions of responsibility. At the time of writing, teaching salary scales ranged from £17,000 to £40,000 but with senior, deputy and head teachers earning much more.

Secretaries' salaries vary according to the type of industry they are employed in, as opposed to whether or not they use languages in their work. Those working for company head offices, large solicitors' practices, in financial services and computing companies earn the highest salaries while those working in advertising, the media and charitable organisations earn the lowest average salaries.

The earnings of self-employed translators and interpreters vary greatly. Some are quite poorly paid while others earn large amounts. Conference interpreters working for international organisations are usually paid on fixed scales. Other people have to work for fees agreed with individual clients – and may have to negotiate their own rates. How much they earn therefore depends on how much work they do – and how quickly. Freelance interpreters are paid by the hour or on a daily rate – £25 plus per hour or between £150 and £300 a day. Freelance translators are often paid by the 1,000 words (on rates varying from £50 to over

£100, depending on the difficulty of the text and their own reputation).

The highest paid linguists are those working in permanent posts for the European institutions, who may earn between £30,000 and £65,000. (Their salaries are paid in local currency, so the exact sterling equivalents fluctuate with exchange rates.)

What are the hours and holidays like?

Again, self-employed linguists decide this largely for themselves. They must work the hours necessary to keep up with client work. If they want to earn a reasonable income they may not be able to turn away new business and they must certainly keep on top of the workload produced by present clients. Some people actually find that they have to give themselves more time off (breaks from work rather than holidays) than they might think. Interpreters, for instance, could not work for days on end without breaks because of the stress of the job. Tourist guides might like to work seven days a week in the busy season but usually find that they need to rest their voices.

Teachers in state schools get twelve or thirteen weeks 'holiday' each year but any teacher will tell you that these weeks balance against the long hours spent in marking and preparing work during term time and that part of the holidays is spent in the same way.

In many other jobs, people work a fairly standard 35–40 hour week with regular office hours – but with overtime when necessary. Most employers in Britain give their staff between four and five weeks annual holiday plus bank holidays – some more – some less.

Will I meet the public?

In some jobs, yes, in others no. Also, it depends on how you define 'the public'. You might be in a job where you constantly meet different groups of people but who are drawn from particular professions or businesses. The jobs which would give you the most contact with the general public would be those in travel, transport, tourism and leisure. In these cases you will often need to deal with both your customers/clients and non-English speaking locals, which is no small challenge.

Are the prospects good for my career?

Opportunities to use languages as a primary skill are limited. Interpreting is a very small field. It is estimated that only a few thousand people throughout the world earn a living from interpreting alone. There are very few full-time posts and most interpreters are freelance. There are more staff posts for translators – with large companies, governments and international organisations – but the majority of translators are also freelance.

The number of jobs in the travel and tourism industries tends to fluctuate with the general economy and the number of people able to spend money on holidays. Jobs are often on a short term or seasonal basis.

Language teachers are much in demand at the moment, and have been for some time. This means that there are currently favourable terms on offer and good prospects for potential language teachers – a situation likely to remain for at least the near future.

Promotion and career development prospects would depend on you to a large extent – on how hard you want to work and what level of responsibility you want to handle. In teaching, for instance, promotion and higher salaries come to people who become heads of department in schools. (Some people hate this idea and want to stay as classroom teachers.)

Self-employed people don't have promotion prospects as such but largely determine the shape of their own careers and earning power.

Some jobs are not well paid – but people do them from interest. It is quite common for people who have just qualified in languages to spend one or more years working in different countries as teachers of English. In some language schools the work is poorly paid and in some countries the work is offered on almost volunteer terms. But the people doing this find rewards other than financial ones.

For the person using languages as a secondary skill, being able to speak them does in general improve career prospects. Job opportunities that require them to deal with people of other nationalities or to travel in the course of their work become possible.

What about training at work?

As a career linguist you would not receive your initial training in languages at work. This is done before you start – you are employed because you already have those skills. You would be given any training necessary to help you do your job though, and to adapt to the employers' methods of work – and you might be sent on refresher courses from time to time. You might also be trained in an additional language.

If you were using languages as an additional skill in a job, then the employer might offer training. If, for instance, you were required to learn a language that you did not already know, they would arrange for you to have tuition. This could be very intensive in some cases. If someone is being sent abroad to live for several years and work in a branch of an organisation in another country, employers often send him or her on a month-long (or longer) intensive language courses at a language school.

Will I be able to work overseas or travel for my job?

Very probably – and certainly while you are still learning your languages.

If the job that you eventually get does not involve you in foreign travel you will still, almost certainly, want to go abroad from time to time to practise and keep your knowledge up-to-date and sharpen your language skills. Teachers often spend part of their holidays abroad either on refresher courses or in general travel.

Not all jobs connected with languages involve travel. Those that do are mainly in travel, tourism, interpreting, and general business and industry (in export, sales and marketing departments). Other people may get the opportunity to travel occasionally in their work.

If travel is not a part of your job, the chance to live abroad for a period may be possible.

That will depend in part on your choice of employer and in part on your own career planning. Some companies have offices in other countries to which staff may be seconded for periods. Alternatively, you can take matters into your own hands and decide to move abroad and look for work.

Finding a job in another country requires some patience – and initiative, because you have to know where to look and how to set about it. There are employment agencies that specialise in overseas placement and the Employment Service, run by the Department for Work and Pensions, has links with counterparts in European Union countries.

You cannot simply move to any country to look for work. The situation will depend on whether there is a shortage there for people with your qualifications or whether they have large numbers of people out of work. Some countries require employers to apply for permission to employ foreigners. However, there is free movement of labour within the member states of the European Union. You do not need any special permission to live and work in one of these countries.

What are the recent developments in this area?

Different languages are coming into prominence. French is still the language most commonly taught in secondary schools but it is not necessarily the one you might use most in a job. Japanese, eastern European languages, Russian and Chinese are all used commercially. Spanish has overtaken German as one of the languages most used in international sales and marketing. Many employers, however, still tend to ask for French – plus one other language. In order of importance these seem at present to be: Spanish, German, Italian – and then the more uncommon languages.

It can make sense to learn two fairly widely spoken European languages followed by a less usual one to give yourself an edge.

Remember that European languages are not spoken only in Europe. French is used in part of Canada and in some African countries, and Spanish in many Central and South American countries. Not only that, but many people in eastern Europe speak German as a second language.

What impact has new technology had on this work?

As the words might suggest, new information and communications technology such as the Internet has had a two-pronged effect on the practices of translating and interpreting.

The growth in the volume and accessibility of information, *from* all countries and available *to* all countries, means that there is the potential for a lot of work for translators. Whether or not this has a significant impact on the translating profession remains to be seen but it could provide you with a number of new opportunities. And it is unlikely that computerised translating programs will do anything to kill of the art of human linguistics.

Secondly, and similarly, more forms of communication – the Internet, email, video conferencing etc. – mean more conflicts of language and opportunities for both translators and interpreters. Again, it remains to be seen how big an impact this will have on the profession, but in theory it should open up a few more avenues for you to pursue.

Could I become famous?

It is not very likely that you will become well known. Have you ever heard of a famous linguist? The reverse is often true. Linguists are anonymous and fade into the background. Quite often when the television news shows two important people meeting, there is a third, utterly forgettable, person standing unobtrusively, near them. This is usually the interpreter!

You could become well-known in your own profession however. People in the field usually know who is the expert in such and such a particular aspect or unusual language.

Could I work independently?

Yes. There are lots of opportunities for independent work. In fact some jobs involving languages positively lend themselves to working alone. Some are actually more possible if you are prepared to work for yourself. Translating and interpreting are two as we have seen. Tourist guides are also usually employed on a daily basis or on short term contracts. Teachers may also work for themselves, giving private lessons or having part-time contracts with more than one school.

How can I find out more about the work?

You can talk to your teachers and careers advisers and look in the publications listed towards the back of this guide, but there is no substitute for talking to people who actually do the job you are interested in, or getting some relevant work experience. Of course, this will be easier in areas like teaching than in the more obscure jobs such as personal interpreter to the President of Burundi, but ask around – you never know. A good place to start is the addresses section at the back of this book. Here you will find contact details for the various organisations and bodies who should be able to help you.

What should I do now to prepare?

Think about the choices you have yet to make regarding subjects and courses. There are several different routes into careers using languages. Learn as many languages as you can. If you can't take more than one or even two for an examination course, does your school or college offer any other courses? Some run beginners courses in languages which students can take in their spare time. Or you could try an evening class. As a general rule of thumb, the more languages you can offer the better. Even if an employer could not use the particular combination you were offering, they would have proof of your ability to learn languages – and might send you on a course at their expense to learn the one(s) needed.

What courses and qualifications are available?

There are a huge number of courses and qualifications available and you should be able to find one to suit your abilities.

Degrees

There are many, many degree courses offered by most universities and colleges of higher education. Lasting four years, a languages degree is usually the first step in a related career, and one course can cover up to three languages.

You need to be careful when you are choosing a degree, making sure that the course content is suitable for you. Some courses are very 'traditional' in their outlook, emphasising literature and related studies with comparatively little time spent on the languages themselves. Others take a more practical approach and feature training in translating and interpreting techniques. There are also a number of courses that combine a language, or languages, with other subjects such as Business Studies or Law. Look in books such as *Degree Course Offers* (published by Trotman) and the UCAS *Big Guide*, as well as in individual university and college prospectuses, for details of the variety of degrees available.

All courses include spending a year abroad, usually as a student, language assistant in a school, or in employment. The idea is that such an experience provides the best way of achieving fluency.

Higher National Diplomas

An alternative to a degree is a Higher National Diploma. HNDs last for two years and are often used as stepping-stones to a full degree course. The emphasis on these courses is usually on business studies or other vocational areas with languages being an additional element.

Postgraduate courses

Postgraduate degrees and diplomas (MA, MSc, PgDip etc.) are generally for individuals who want to go on to become translators or interpreters. Although not always essential, it is common to take such a qualification to enter this type of work. The Institute of Translating and Interpreting has a list of translation and interpreting courses available in the UK on its website.

Vocational qualifications

There are a number of more job-oriented courses available run by colleges and other organisations around the country. They cover a range of languages and abilities and can act as equivalents to traditional A-levels and degrees, as well as qualifying you to take more advanced courses and join certain professional organisations. Vocational qualifications include Vocational A-levels, S/NVQs and various independently run courses (e.g. the Institute of Linguists runs a number of applied language courses at different levels). As with all courses, you need to be careful which you choose, particularly so in the case of privately run qualifications as they can cost a lot of money.

What publications should I look at?

Careers guides

The *A–Z of Careers and Jobs* (Kogan Page)
Careers Using Languages (Kogan Page)
The *Daily Telegraph Guide to Working Abroad* (Kogan Page)
Getting a Job Abroad (How To Books)
Getting a Job in Europe (How To Books)
Getting into Languages (Trotman)
Getting into Tourism (Trotman)
Great Careers for People Interested in Languages (Kogan Page)
How to Make it in the Travel Industry (Virgin)
Teach English as a Foreign Language (How To Books)
Teaching English Abroad (Vacation Work Publications)
Working in Languages (COIC)

Language learning

Degree Course Offers (Trotman)
Directory of Further Education (CRAC/Hobsons)
Directory of University and College Entrance (Trotman)
Getting into Europe (Trotman)
How to Choose Your Postgraduate Course (Trotman)
www.language-learning.net
Taking a Year Off (Trotman)
University and College Entrance aka the *Big Guide* (UCAS)

Which addresses will help me?

Association of Translation Companies
Suite 10–11
Kent House
87 Regent Street
London W1R 7HF
020 7437 0007
www.atc.org.uk

Centre for Information on Language Teaching and Research
20 Bedfordbury
London WC2N 4LB
020 7379 5110
www.cilt.org.uk

Institute of Linguists
Saxon House
48 Southwark Street
London SE1 1UN
020 7940 3100
www.iol.org.uk

Institute of Translation & Interpreting
Exchange House
494 Midsummer Boulevard
Central Milton Keynes
MK9 2EA
01908 255 905
www.iti.org.uk

Teaching & Projects Abroad
Gerrard House
Rustington
West Sussex BN16 1AW
01903 859911
www.teaching-abroad.co.uk

The Translators Association
84 Drayton Gardens
London SW10 9SB
020 7373 6642

The following organisations will be able to advise you on what language courses are available to you.

Alliance Française
1 Dorset Square
London NW1 6PU
020 7723 6439
www.alliancefrancaise.org.uk

Association for Language Learning
150 Railway Terrace
Rugby CV21 3HN
01788 546 443
www.languagelearn.co.uk

**Cambridge Advisory Service
for Language Courses
Abroad**
Rectory Lane
Kingston
Cambridge CB3 7NL
01223 264 089

**Central Bureau for
International Education and
Training**
10 Spring Gardens
London SW1A 2BN
020 7389 4004
www.centralbureau.org.uk
which also run the Socrates
programme in the UK at
www.socrates-uk.net

CESA Languages Abroad
Western House
Malpas
Truro TR1 1SQ
01872 225 300
www.cesalanguages.com

Goethe Institut (German)
50 Princes Gate
Exhibition Road
London SW7 2PH
020 7596 4000
www.goethe.de

Institut Français
17 Queensberry Place
London SW7 2DT
020 7073 1350
www.institut.ambafrance.org.uk

Instituto Cervantes (Spanish)
102 Eaton Square
London SW1W 9AN
020 7235 0353
www.cervantes.es

Italian Cultural Institute
39 Belgrave Square
London SW1X 8NX
020 7235 1461
www.italcultur.org.uk

**Universities & Colleges
Admissions Service (UCAS)**
Rosehill
New Barn Lane
Cheltenham GL52 3LZ
01242 222 444
www.ucas.com

Q&A